324171

17.68
NBS
8/04
z

MW00901996

WITHDRAWN

TURTLES

Please visit our web site at: www.garethstevens.com
For a free color catalog describing Gareth Stevens Publishing's
list of high-quality books and multimedia programs, call
1-800-542-2595 (USA) or 1-800-387-3178 (Canada).
Gareth Stevens Publishing's fax: (414) 332-3567.

Library of Congress Cataloging-in-Publication Data available upon request from publisher.
Fax (414) 336-0157 for the attention of the Publishing Records Department.

ISBN 0-8368-4123-9

This edition first published in 2004 by
Gareth Stevens Publishing
A World Almanac Education Group Company
330 West Olive Street, Suite 100
Milwaukee, Wisconsin 53212 USA

Editorial and design: Tucker Slingsby Ltd., London
Gareth Stevens series editor: Catherine Gardner
Gareth Stevens art direction: Tammy Gruenewald

Picture Credits
NHPA — Linda and Brian Pitkin: cover, title page, 6-7, 14; Jany Sauvanet: 9; Ken
    Griffiths: 11; Pavel German: 15; B. Jones and M. Shimlock: 16; A.N.T. Photo Library:
    17; Pete Atkinson: 21, 24-25; Martin Harvey: 29.
Oxford Scientific Films — Gerard Soury: 7; Mark Jones: 8; David B. Fleetham: 9, 15,
    22-23; Victoria McCormick: 10; Howard Hall: 12-13, 18; Kathie Atkinson: 13; Zig
    Leszczynski: 13; Olivier Grunewald: 19; Paul Kay: 20; David Cayless: 21; Daniel J.
    Cox: 23; Jack Dermid: 23; Tui de Roy: 26; Tom Ulrich: 27; Michael Sewell: 28.

Printed in the United States of America

1 2 3 4 5 6 7 8 9 08 07 06 05 04

TURTLES

Gareth Stevens Publishing
A WORLD ALMANAC EDUCATION GROUP COMPANY

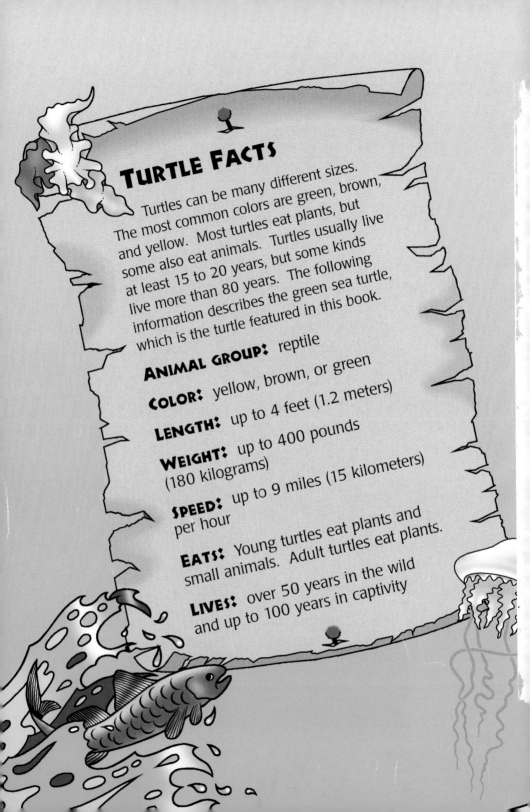

Turtle Facts

Turtles can be many different sizes. The most common colors are green, brown, and yellow. Most turtles eat plants, but some also eat animals. Turtles usually live at least 15 to 20 years, but some kinds live more than 80 years. The following information describes the green sea turtle, which is the turtle featured in this book.

ANIMAL GROUP: reptile

COLOR: yellow, brown, or green

LENGTH: up to 4 feet (1.2 meters)

WEIGHT: up to 400 pounds (180 kilograms)

SPEED: up to 9 miles (15 kilometers) per hour

EATS: Young turtles eat plants and small animals. Adult turtles eat plants.

LIVES: over 50 years in the wild and up to 100 years in captivity

CONTENTS

Words that appear in the glossary
are printed in **boldface** type the
first time they occur in the text.

A Closer Look

Turtles belong to a big group of animals called reptiles. Snakes and lizards are reptiles, too. Reptiles have scaly skin, and most of them hatch from eggs. They are also cold-blooded, which means they need the Sun's warmth to give them the energy to move. Very few kinds of reptiles live in the ocean, but sea turtles are one of them. Most other kinds of turtles live on land or in **freshwater**.

I have tough scales that protect my head and my body.

My front flippers help me swim through the water in my ocean home.

My shell protects my soft body. It has a top half and a bottom half.

My body shape is streamlined for gliding smoothly through the sea.

Fast Flippers

Sea turtles are slow and clumsy on land but speedy and graceful in the water. When they swim, they move their large, flat flippers up and down like wings, and they can paddle this way for hours. One type of sea turtle, known as the leatherback turtle, can swim as fast as 20 miles (32 kilometers) per hour.

- A turtle's shell is made up of lots of bony plates. The plates are covered with a layer of hard scales that are called scutes.

- A turtle's top shell is called a carapace. The carapace is shaped like a dome.

- The flat shell underneath a turtle's body is called the plastron.

- A turtle's backbone and ribs are on the inside of its shell.

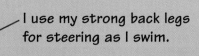

I use my strong back legs for steering as I swim.

My webbed back feet are great for swimming and for digging in the sand.

7

Sea turtles are well **adapted** to their underwater homes. They have good eyesight, which helps them find their way around the ocean and look for food. Many types of sea turtles also have a good sense of smell. Turtles do not have teeth, but they do have tough, sharp jaws that can cut through plants and snap up small animals. A type of sea turtle known as the green sea turtle uses its jaws to pull up tasty grasses that grow on the ocean floor.

LONG SLEEP

Cold-blooded animals need the warmth of the Sun to heat their blood and give them energy, so they cannot live in very cold places. Although turtles do not live in places that are cold all year long, they do live in parts of the world that are cold for just a few months of the year. During the cold-weather months, food is hard to find, so, to survive, turtles **hibernate**. They bury their bodies in sand or mud or under plants and go into a deep sleep until warm weather returns.

I can see well underwater. Special, heavy eyelids protect my eyes.

I hear through flat disks behind my eyes. My ears do not stick out from my head like human ears do.

The nostrils at the tip of my nose are small, but I have a good sense of smell.

I do not have any teeth, but my sharp jaws can cut through tough plants.

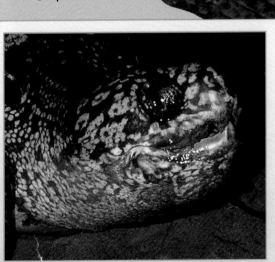

TURTLE TEARS

When sea turtles are on land, they look as if they are crying — but they are not sad! Sea turtles drink salt water from the ocean. All of the water they drink can put too much salt in their bodies, which makes them sick. The extra salt leaves their bodies through their eyes in the form of many very salty tears.

Home, Sweet Home

Sea turtles live in seas and oceans all over the world. The leatherback sea turtle can be found as far north as the cold waters around Canada. Sea turtles spend most of their lives swimming underwater, but because they breathe air, they must come to the surface now and then. An adult green sea turtle can swim underwater for up to five hours between breaths.

Where in the World?

More than 250 **species** of turtles live on Earth, and they have adapted to many different **habitats**, including deserts, oceans, rivers, and rain forests. Turtles live in nearly every part of the world except the icy Arctic and Antarctic areas around the North and South Poles. **Fossils** show that the first turtles lived on Earth more than 200 million years ago. Turtles were around even before dinosaurs!

STRETCHY NECK

The snake-necked turtle lives in shallow rivers in Australia. It can lie on the river bottom and stretch its long neck to the surface of the water to breathe. When it wants to tuck its head under its shell, the snake-necked turtle must bend its neck sideways.

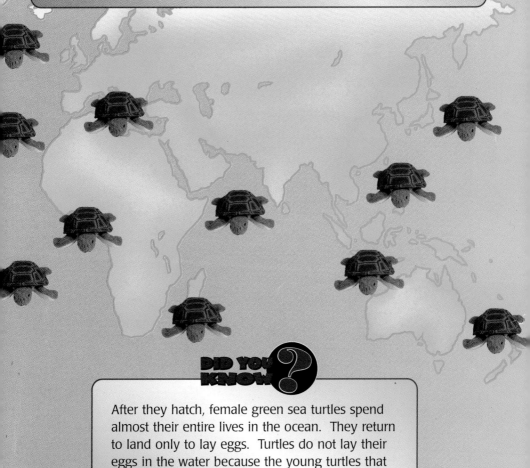

DID YOU KNOW?

After they hatch, female green sea turtles spend almost their entire lives in the ocean. They return to land only to lay eggs. Turtles do not lay their eggs in the water because the young turtles that are growing in the eggs need air to breathe.

NEIGHBORS

Some green sea turtles live in the Caribbean Sea. The clear, warm water is the perfect home for a sea turtle. The water is shallow, with lots of sea grass growing on the seafloor. Many other creatures live in the Caribbean Sea, too. Millions of plants, tiny animals, and jellyfish float at the surface. Fish swim through the water and around **coral**. Octopuses and squid lurk in the shadows, watching for passing **prey**.

FLOATING LIONS

Jellyfish may have no bones or brains, but they are deadly **predators**! They trap small creatures in their **tentacles** and sting them to death. A kind of jellyfish known as the lion's mane jellyfish has a watery, see-through body, so it is hard for other animals to see it floating by.

LET'S HIDE

Many fish have shapes or colors that help them hide from their enemies. The bright colors of the beautiful queen angelfish blend in with the colors of ocean coral.

The sea horse can change color to blend in with its surroundings. This tiny fish is different from most other kinds of fish, in several ways. It swims upright and can hold on to sea grasses with its tail, and the male gives birth to the babies!

INK OUT!

A reef squid (*left*) hides in the coral, waiting to pounce on passing fish and **shellfish**. While it waits for its prey, it must also watch out for predators. This squid can change its color to match nearby coral, making it harder for its enemies to find it. The reef squid can also squirt a black liquid, called ink, at an attacker, then escape in the inky darkness.

THE FAMILY

Sea turtles live by themselves most of the time. They may group together at a good feeding ground, but each goes its own way after eating. Also, male and female turtles come together to mate, but then, the male stays in the sea while the female struggles onto the beach to lay her eggs. Some kinds of sea turtles **migrate** 1,000 miles (1,600 km) or more to lay their eggs on the beaches were they were born.

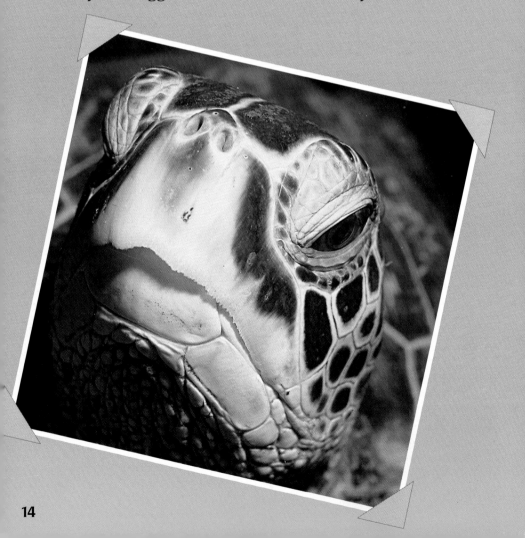

Sea turtles usually lay eggs at night. To lay her eggs, a female turtle uses her huge front flippers to drag herself up the beach. She must lay the eggs above the high **tide** line, or the water could wash them away. On the beach, the turtle digs a hole with her back legs and lays about one hundred eggs in the hole. Then she covers the eggs with sand and heads back to the sea. She stays in the same area for a few weeks, laying several groups of eggs.

RUN!

Sea turtles lay lots of eggs because most of their young do not survive. Predators sniff out and dig up many of the eggs before they hatch. The young, or hatchlings, that do survive must cross the beach and race for the ocean. On the way to the water, birds and crabs gobble up most of them. Out of one hundred hatchlings, only one or two survive the first year.

Baby File

Birth

Sea turtle eggs hatch about sixty days after the female lays them. A hatchling uses a special tooth on its jaw to break its eggshell. Then it digs itself out of the sand, drags itself to the sea, and swims out to deep water. A green sea turtle hatchling is about 2 inches (5 centimeters) long.

Six Months to Three Years

Young green sea turtles do not swim well, so they often float on beds of seaweed and eat the tiny creatures that live there. When the turtles grow bigger, they can swim to the feeding grounds. Their shells are still soft, so young turtles are easy prey for many kinds of fish.

Boy or Girl?

Turtles sometimes lay their eggs in shady spots on the beach and sometimes in hot, sunny spots. Scientists think that the temperature of the sand where an egg develops may play a part in whether the egg becomes a male or a female turtle. They believe that the hotter the sand is, the more likely the turtle will be a female.

Five to Fifteen Years

As sea turtles grow older, they stop eating small animals and eat only plants. They graze on the sea grass and seaweed that grow on the ocean floor and may swim long distances to find good feeding areas. Sea turtles spend most of their time in shallow, sheltered waters. They become adults when they are about fifteen years old.

LIFE IN THE SEA

During its lifetime, a sea turtle swims millions of miles (kilometers). It makes its first journey as a tiny hatchling, when it crawls across the beach and swims out to sea. As an adult, the sea turtle travels from its feeding grounds to the beach where it was born, safely buries its eggs in the sand, then returns to its feeding grounds. No one knows how a sea turtle finds its way over such long distances. Each of a turtle's trips, or migrations, can take up to two years to complete.

TURTLE TRIPS

A kind of sea turtle called a loggerhead lives in the Pacific Ocean around Mexico and California. Loggerheads feed on the red crabs that live in that part of the ocean. When loggerheads lay their eggs, however, some of them look for nesting spots on the other side of the ocean, which is a trip of more than 9,300 miles (15,000 km).

Long-Distance Leatherback

The leatherback turtle gets its name from its rubbery, leathery-looking shell. This turtle's large size and barrel-like shape help it dive deeper, travel farther, and swim in colder water than other kinds of sea turtles. Leatherbacks live in the open ocean, as far north as Alaska and as far south as the southern tip of Africa.

Some green sea turtles take only a short trip around the coast to lay their eggs. Other green sea turtles swim up to 1,250 miles (2,000 km), from South America to tiny Ascension Island in the Atlantic Ocean.

FAVORITE FOODS

Turtles of many different sizes, shapes, and colors live in many different habitats. What they eat depends on where they live. The turtles that live in freshwater eat animals. Some sea turtles, such as green sea turtles, eat plants. Other sea turtles eat jellyfish or crabs. A turtle's jaws and mouth are adapted to the food it finds in its habitat.

GREENS, PLEASE!

As babies, green sea turtles eat plants and animals. As adults, they eat only plants. Green sea turtles snap up seaweed and sea grass, both of which can be hard to pull up from the seabed and to chew. These turtles have sharp, jagged jaws to handle their tough food.

DID YOU KNOW?

- Turtles can go for months without eating or drinking. They live on special, fatty lumps in their bodies.

- Sea turtles sleep either at the surface of the water or on the ocean floor in shallow water.

MEATY MEAL

A horseshoe crab is a good meal for a loggerhead turtle. This sea turtle has strong jaws that can crunch through tough shellfish.

JUICY JELLY

A leatherback turtle eats jellyfish. To snap up its prey, this type of turtle has jaws that are shaped like scissors. At night, jellyfish swim to the bottom of the sea, but they are not safe there. Leatherbacks will dive more than 3,000 feet (900 meters) for a juicy jellyfish dinner!

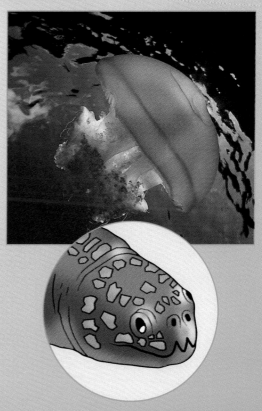

DANGER!

A sea turtle cannot pull its body into its shell, so it depends on its large size and strong swimming to keep it safe. The hard shell of an adult turtle will protect it from most enemies, except humans and fierce sharks, but a baby turtle has many enemies, including birds, crabs, and snakes, on land, and fish, dolphins, and sharks, in the water. Many sea turtle hatchlings do not survive.

SHARK ATTACK!

The tiger shark is a ferocious predator. Its super-sharp teeth can slice through even tough turtle shells. The shark bites into adult turtles but swallows baby turtles whole.

GHOSTLY HUNTER

A ghost crab hides in its burrow and waits for a turtle hatchling to pass by. When a hatchling gets close, the crab grabs it by its flipper and drags the young turtle off to eat it.

NIGHT HUNTER

Raccoons hunt at night. Some of them roam beaches, trying to sniff out a meal. When a raccoon smells a nest of turtle eggs, it digs up the sand and steals the eggs. When it sees hatchlings crawling toward the ocean, the raccoon gobbles up as many as it can catch.

A Turtle's Day

6:00 AM

The Sun started to rise, but the water still felt cool. Green sea turtles like me prefer warmer water, so I stayed under my rocky shelf and snoozed.

8:00 AM

I woke up hungry and swam over to some sea grass that was growing nearby. I had a good feed. Sea grass is my favorite food!

10:00 AM

The Sun felt hot, so I decided to warm up at the surface of the water. I soaked up sunshine until it was time for lunch.

12:00 NOON

I ate so much sea grass that I felt full and lazy. It was time for a rest. Tomorrow, I will begin my journey to the beach where I lay my eggs.

2:00 PM

I was still resting when a little cleaner fish swam up to me. Cleaner fish eat the tiny animals that live on turtles. We get cleaned, and the fish get a good meal!

3:00 PM

I swam to a spot where I knew I would find plenty of food. Before long, I saw sea grass swaying in the water.

4:00 PM

Lots of green sea turtles gathered at the feeding ground. We greeted each other with a grunt, then started eating. I cut off chunks of sea grass with my sharp jaws and munched it up.

5:00 PM

I saw a shape moving toward us. It was a tiger shark! I stopped eating and stayed still. I blend in well with my grassy home, so the shark did not see me. It looked around, then swam away.

8:00 PM

The Sun had gone down, but the water at the surface was still warm. I ate once more before swimming under a rocky ledge for a snooze.

12:00 MIDNIGHT

I needed to come up for air, so I decided to go for a little swim. A full Moon bathed the sea with its bright light. I snacked on some seaweed before going back to sleep.

4:00 AM

The Sun will rise in another hour or so, and I will have a big meal. Then, I'll swim down the coast. I'll eat along the way because, when I reach the open ocean, I won't be able to feed again. I'll have to live off my fat. The journey to lay my eggs is very long.

RELATIVES

Not all members of the turtle family live in the sea. Some kinds of turtles live in rivers and lakes, and others live on land. Terrapins are close relatives of turtles. They look a lot like sea turtles, but they live in freshwater and on land. Tortoises are also related to turtles. Tortoises have high, domed shells and live on land. Because tortoises have heavy shells and big bodies, they move very slowly.

GENTLE GIANT

Giant tortoises are found only on a few islands. They can grow to be more than 3 feet (1 m) long and weigh as much as five people weigh together. Giant tortoises **browse** on plants. Some kinds of tortoises even eat prickly cactus!

- Most kinds of turtles can pull their heads into their shells for protection, but sea turtles cannot. Their heads are too big to pull into their shells.

- The terrapin gets its name from a Native American word meaning "little turtle."

SNAP!

A snapping turtle has strong jaws for hunting fish and other water animals. This kind of turtle does not hide inside its shell. It depends more on its jaws than its shell for protection. The jaws of a snapping turtle are strong enough to snap off a human's toe!

RIVER DWELLER

A diamondback terrapin sleeps in the mud! It lives in rivers near the Gulf and Atlantic coasts of North America. Terrapins usually **bask** in the warm sun during the day but bury themselves in soft mud at night.

HUMANS AND TURTLES

Turtles, terrapins, and tortoises are well-known animals throughout the world. In many countries, people believe that these long-lived creatures bring wisdom and good fortune, and, in parts of the world, turtle meat and eggs are popular foods. In some places, people kill turtles for their shells. People also force turtles out of their habitats by damaging natural areas. Some species of turtles are now facing **extinction**.

SHINY SHELLS

Shells of tortoises and turtles, including the hawksbill turtle, are often polished to make a material called tortoiseshell. This material is used to make or decorate combs, jewelry, and boxes. The species of turtles used to make tortoiseshell are now very rare.

- The green sea turtle is used to make turtle soup.

- In the past, sailors caught sea turtles and kept them aboard ships. When the sailors were far from land and had no fresh food left, they ate the turtles.

- Thousands of sea turtles drown each year by getting stuck in fishing nets.

HELP THE TURTLES

Some people are helping to save sea turtles by learning more about how these turtles live and behave. By understanding where, when, and how sea turtles nest, develop, and survive, people can better protect these amazing animals.

ANCIENT TURTLES

Turtles have been on Earth much longer than humans have. The earliest type of turtle, known as Proganochelys, lived 210 million years ago. Its shell had the same pattern of bones and plates as the turtles of today. A type of sea turtle called Archelon was the biggest ever known. It was 13 feet (4 m) long. The Archelon turtle lived over 65 million years ago.

GLOSSARY

ADAPTED
Changed to be better-suited to the conditions of a place.

BASK
To rest comfortably in the warmth of the Sun.

BROWSE
To feed, or graze, on living plants.

CORAL
A hard substance made from the skeletons of tiny sea creatures that collect on the ocean floor.

EXTINCTION
The state of having died out completely as a species and no longer existing.

FOSSILS
The remains of animals or plants from times long past, which have been preserved or embedded in rocks and minerals.

FRESHWATER
The natural water of most inland lakes and rivers, which does not have the large amounts of salt and other minerals found in seawater.

HABITATS
The natural settings in which plants and animals live.

HIBERNATE
To spend a long period of cold weather in a kind of deep sleep, during which all of the body functions slow down.

MIGRATE
To travel from one place to another to find a new food supply or warmer temperatures or to reproduce.

PREDATORS
Animals that hunt other animals for food.

PREY
Animals that another animal hunts and kills for food.

SHELLFISH
Sea animals, such as clams, crabs, and lobsters, that have hard coverings, or shells, protecting their bodies.

SPECIES
Groups of animals in which the members of a group have many of the same physical features and behaviors and can mate with each other to produce offspring.

TENTACLES
The long, flexible, grasping arms of animals such as squid and octopuses.

TIDE
The movement of seawater, especially the rise and fall that occurs twice a day due to the Moon's alternating pulls on water and solid earth.

INDEX